Judo
柔道

Contents

Written by Rachel Blackburn

Introduction

Judo is a sport that hundreds of thousands of people all around the world are involved in. There are many reasons why people become involved in judo. The main reason is to take part in a body-contact sport in a controlled environment.

Other reasons for taking up judo –

- Men, women, and children of all ages can participate.

- People who are visually and/or hearing impaired can participate.

- People can enter competitions or just fight for recreation.

- There are many levels of involvement. When a judo fighter stops fighting they can continue the sport by coaching, refereeing, or managing teams.

- There is an opportunity to compete at the highest level because judo is an Olympic sport.

The History of Judo

Judo comes from Japan. Many years ago, in Japan, most people were not allowed to carry weapons. Instead they used their bodies to defend themselves.

In 1882, a man named Professor Jigoro Kano started what people now know as the modern sport of judo. When Professor Jigoro Kano was young, his family moved to the country. Because he was small and new to the area, it was easy for bullies to pick on him. But Professor Jigoro Kano fought back. He fought the bullies using moves from a martial art called *jujitsu*. The bullies respected his fighting ability and soon stopped picking on him.

Japan

Professor Jigoro Kano

As he grew up, Professor Jigoro Kano developed his own moves from jujitsu moves and called the new sport *judo*. Soon he began teaching judo to people all over Japan. From there, judo spread throughout the world.

Inner thigh reaping throw (Called *Uchi-mata* in Japanese)

Do not try any of the moves in this book, unless you are a qualified and registered judo player!

Professor Jigoro Kano's motto was *maximum efficiency, minimum effort*. Today this motto guides all judo fighters, who are called *judokas*. In a judo fight, judokas rely on skill, strength, and speed, but never on weapons.

Judo Vocabulary

Japanese	English
dan	*grade (black belt)*
dojo	*practice hall*
gatame	*hold*
judo	*the gentle way*
judogi	*judo uniform*
judoka	*judo fighter*
kyu	*class*
randori	*free practice*
sensei	*instructor/teacher*
shiai	*competition*
uke	*partner for practice*
zori	*slippers/shoes*

Rules

People involved in judo learn to enjoy their sport within a set of rules.

These rules teach judokas how to –

- Practice judo safely.
- Respect themselves, other judokas, and the training hall (*dojo*).
- Keep their personal hygiene to a standard required for participating in a body-contact sport.

Some rules that judokas learn are –

- Bow when entering or leaving the dojo.
- Bow at the start and end of *randori* or *shiai.*
- Never hurt anyone while fighting, especially if that person is of a lower rank.
- Keep fingernails and toenails short to avoid injury on the opponent (*uke*).
- Do not wear footwear on the mats – wear slippers (*zori*).
- Do not eat or drink in the dojo.
- After the first grade, wear a judo uniform (*judogi*).

What to Wear

Beginner judokas can wear loose clothing like a comfortable tracksuit. Judokas must not wear clothing with buttons, zips, or buckles because these could cause an injury. When judokas get more experienced, they wear a special outfit called a judogi.

A judogi is made of cotton. It is a loose pair of white pants and a long-sleeved top. The pants are tied with a drawstring. The top is tied with a belt. There are no buckles, buttons, or pockets that might cause injury. A judogi should always be clean and tidy.

Training for Judo

People have to be physically fit for judo and be prepared to train hard. A training session usually lasts one to two hours. Children and social judokas train two to three times a week. Judokas training for major competitions can train up to twice a day, six days a week.

Judokas stretch before training

The judo teacher (*sensei*) starts a lesson with a warm-up. During the warm-up, the students loosen their muscles by doing exercises and playing fitness games.

The sensei then shows the students some new moves and techniques. The students do the same move over and over until they are comfortable with that move. Then, the students learn another move.

One-arm shoulder throw
(Called *Ippon-seoi-nage* in Japanese)

13

After the students have practiced the new moves, they fight. In judo, fighting is called *randori*.

Randori can be fighting on the ground, standing up, or a combination of both.

Fighting (*randori*) standing up

When students fight standing up, they try to get their opponents off balance and throw them onto the ground. If the students get their opponents on the ground, they then try to apply a hold down.

Fighting (*randori*) on the ground

Judo Moves

There are five components that make up judo. These are throws, hold downs, armlocks, strangles, and chokes. Strangles, chokes, and armlocks are not taught until the judokas are 14–15 years old and experienced fighters.

Before students learn how to fight, they learn how to fall safely. Instructors (*sensei*) show students how to fall correctly with their arms stretched out so that they do not hurt themselves.

There are four different ways that judokas can breakfall. They can fall backward, to forward, either side, or do a rolling breakfall.

Backward breakfall

Sideway breakfall

Rolling breakfall

Holds

There are many different holds. A hold down occurs when one judoka has their opponent's shoulders pinned to the mat.

In the hold shown below, the judoka on top is leaning on their opponent's body. They use one hand as the free arm and the other around the head to hold the opponent down. The opponent is now unable to move. The judoka being held down will tap the uke on top twice, or the mat, to admit defeat and end the fight.

Scarf hold (Called *Kesa-gatame* in Japanese)

Side-locking four-corner hold
(Called *Yoko-shiho-gatame*
in Japanese)

Fighting for the dominant position

19

Armlocks

There are many different armlocks. Armlocks are performed by bending the opponent's arm so that they cannot move. An armlock occurs when one judoka applies pressure to their opponent's elbow joint. The pain causes the opponent to tap twice to admit defeat.

A judoka can win a fight quickly by applying an armlock to an opponent.

Entangled armlock
(Called *Ude-garami* in Japanese)

Cross armlock
(Called *Ude-hishigi-juji-gatame* in Japanese)

Strangles and Chokes

There are many different strangles and chokes. A strangle cuts off blood to the brain. A choke stops the air flow in and out of the windpipe. As with an armlock, a judoka can win a fight instantly by applying a strangle or a choke. When the opponent realizes that a strangle or choke has been applied, they will tap twice to admit defeat.

Normal cross lock
(Called *Nami-juji-jime* in Japanese)

Judo Grading System

Judokas' level of skill is shown by the color of their belt. The color tells how advanced they are.

When people first start training in judo, they wear a white belt. This tells people that they are a beginner. When judokas start to become skilled, the sensei invites them to take part in a grading exam. During the exam, the judoka has to perform judo moves to the best of their ability. They do not fight. If the judoka passes the exam, they are given the next belt.

To move from a brown to a black belt, a judoka needs to have won points in many competitions as well as being able to perform the individual moves in an examination. There are 12 different levels of black belt. These are called *dans*. When judokas have their sixth dan, they may wear a red and white striped belt. Ninth, tenth, and eleventh dans may wear a red belt and twelfth dan may wear an extra-wide white belt. Few judokas have achieved a tenth dan. Professor Jigoro Kano is the only judoka ever to have reached twelfth dan.

Belt Gradings

12th dan

9th dan – 11th dan

6th dan – 8th dan

1st dan – 5th dan

Dan grades

---

black　(1st dan)

brown　(1st kyu)

blue　(2nd kyu)

green　(3rd kyu)

orange　(4th kyu)

yellow　(5th kyu)

white　(6th kyu)

Kyu grades

Competitions

Judokas may want to test their skills by entering a competition. Competitions have different skill levels, from club to national tournaments to the Olympic games. These competitions are weight related, so judokas hardly ever fight anyone who is much heavier or lighter than they are.

Men's Weight Divisions	Women's Weight Divisions
Under these Weights	Under these Weights
132 pounds (60 kg)	106 pounds (48 kg)
146 pounds (66 kg)	115 pounds (52 kg)
161 pounds (73 kg)	126 pounds (57 kg)
179 pounds (81 kg)	139 pounds (63 kg)
198 pounds (90 kg)	154 pounds (70 kg)
220 pounds (100 kg)	172 pounds (78 kg)
Over this Weight	Over this Weight
220 pounds (100 kg)	172 pounds (78 kg)

Judo competitions are held in stadiums where more than one fight usually takes place at a time. Many people attend competitions to watch and support the judokas.

Four judo fights taking place at the same time

Judo fights take place on a green mat area. There is a red strip around each mat. Judokas are not allowed to stand on the red strip while they are competing. The red strip is known as the danger zone, set aside for safety reasons.

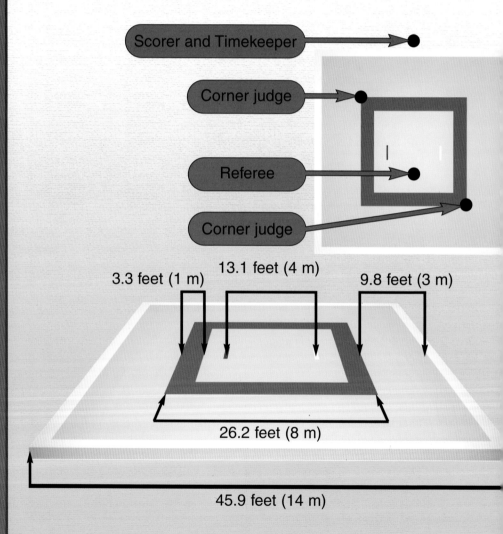

Scorer and Timekeeper

Corner judge

Referee

Corner judge

3.3 feet (1 m)

13.1 feet (4 m)

9.8 feet (3 m)

26.2 feet (8 m)

45.9 feet (14 m)

There are two corner judges, a referee, a timekeeper, and a scorer for each judo competition. A fight can last up to four minutes for women and five minutes for men. A judo match can be won in as little as 25 seconds with a hold down, or as little as 2 seconds with a throw.

This corner judge is watching a women's competition fight.

Judokas score points when they demonstrate or perform a successful move or technique.

Judokas can win by –

- Obtaining more points than their opponent by scoring higher or earning more points from throwing techniques. Throws are also scored differently, depending on which part of the body the person falls on first, and how much speed and power is put into the technique. An automatic win occurs when one opponent throws the other flat on his or her back, cleanly and precisely.

- Obtaining more points than their opponent through scoring higher or earning more points from hold downs. Hold down points depend on the time that the hold down was valid for – up to 25 seconds for an automatic win. Before this time, smaller points are given depending on how long the hold was applied for before being broken out of.

- Forcing a submission from their opponent while applying a strangle, choke, or armlock.

If neither contestant scores points, the judges will decide who attacked the most and that person is the winner.

The referee signals to the winner of the fight.

Benefits of Judo

Judo is a sport that people of all ages and walks of life can enjoy.

Although it is a tough body-contact sport, judo takes place in an environment that is controlled to protect participants from any injury. Regular judo training ensures that participants are physically and mentally fit, and the variety of moves contribute to flexibility, strength, and balance.

The judoka in blue is trying to score points in ground-work techniques.

People can participate in judo at different levels. They can fight socially or at competitions. They can become coaches, referees, judges, and timekeepers.

In judo, there are strict rules governing fights and the way people behave generally. The rules cover areas such as respect for people, personal hygiene, and safety. Participants are encouraged to take these rules and incorporate them into their everyday living.

The judoka in white throws his opponent in a competition fight.

Index